Spotlight on Reading

Cause and Effect
Grades 3–4

Frank Schaffer

An imprint of Carson-Dellosa Publishing LLC
Greensboro, North Carolina

Credits

Layout and Cover Design: Van Harris

Development House: The Research Masters

Cover Photo: Image Copyright Dmitriy Shironosov, 2011 Used under license from Shutterstock.com

 This book has been correlated to state, common core state, national, and Canadian provincial standards. Visit *www.carsondellosa.com* to search for and view its correlations to your standards

Frank Schaffer

An imprint of Carson-Dellosa Publishing LLC

PO Box 35665

Greensboro, NC 27425 USA

www.carsondellosa.com

ISBN 978-16-099-6484-9

05-118147784

About the Book

Cause and Effect is designed to apply a cross-curricular approach to the development of cause and effect skills. Due to the ease of confusing cause and effect with other reading comprehension skills, such as sequencing and predicting, this book is written with a focus on offering pure cause and effect activities that use clue words, such as why, because, so, and since. Additionally, character skills are enhanced as students work through practical life applications to examine consequences of actions through critical thinking.

Students with a wide range of abilities will find this book valuable. Activities are written to guide students carefully, yet challenge them to move forward based on personal ability. Critical thinking skills are fostered for all students through cause and effect activities. Students should come away from the book with a renewed respect for their ability to analyze cause and effect in curriculum areas, as well as in their lives outside the classroom.

• •

Table of Contents

It Happened Because . . .

Each picture on the left shows a cause. Each picture on the right shows an effect. Draw a line from each cause to the correct effect.

• •

1.

The boy left the bathroom when the water was running . . .

a.

. . . so the bathtub overflowed.

2.

The girl put too many toys in the sailboat . . .

b.

. . . so the pond froze and we went skating.

3.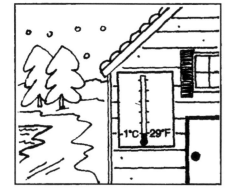

It was a very cold day today . . .

c.

. . . so the sailboat sank.

Sara's Bad Day

Read each pair of sentences. Label each sentence as the cause or effect.

1. Sara watched a scary move on television. _____
   Sara could not sleep at night. _____

2. Sara was late for school. _____
   Sara got up late. _____

3. Sara had to do her homework at recess. _____
   Sara forgot her homework. _____

4. Sara left her lunch ticket at home. _____
   Sara had to wait in the lost ticket line. _____

5. Sara felt better. _____
   On her way home, Sara told a friend about her bad day. _____

6. That night, Sara watched a comedy. _____
   Sara laughed. _____

7. Sara got a good night's sleep. _____
   Sara went to bed on time. _____

5

Camp Days

Read the letter. Answer the cause and effect questions on the next page.

Dear Grandma,

Thank you for saving up to send me to camp. I love the tennis classes! But I miss the tennis court at the rec center at home. I also miss the tennis matches we always play on Saturday. I miss you, Gran.

The food here is not very good, but the people who sit at my table are really nice. I'd really like to gulp down a frozen yogurt from the corner store right about now.

I'm going to ask my friends to take pictures of me tomorrow when we ride our horses. I hardly ever see horses in the city. Getting to ride them is one of the best parts of camp! I wish I could ride horses every day.

I can't wait to see you when camp is over. I know I'll miss my new friends, but I'll write to them a lot.

Love,
Tasha

Name _____

In the box on the left, list things that cause Tasha to like camp. In the box on the right, list things that cause Tasha to miss home.

★ Cause Match

Draw a line to match each cause with the correct effect.

Cause

1. The chain on the bicycle broke.

2. The students worked with chemicals in science class.

3. The computer stopped working.

4. The water pipe broke.

5. The dog jumped out of the soapy washtub.

6. The temperature dropped to 30° F (-1° C).

7. The flash on the camera did not work.

Effect

a. A waterspout shot up out of a manhole.

b. They wore safety goggles to protect their eyes.

c. Suds splashed all over the porch.

d. The wheels would not turn.

e. The photographs turned out dark.

f. The screen went blank.

g. We could see our breath in the air.

Effect Match

Read the effects outside the rectangle. Read the causes inside the rectangle. Draw a line to match each effect to the correct cause.

a. It turned green.

b. The rocks became smooth.

c. It broke.

d. The cake burned.

e. They popped.

f. They would not bounce.

g. Mom could not drive us to the store.

h. The leaves wilted.

1. The car ran out of gas.

2. The oven was too hot when we were baking.

3. Water ran across the rocks for many years.

4. He left the heads of lettuce on the counter for two days.

5. She stretched the rubber band too far.

6. Mom touched pins to the balloons.

7. We mixed yellow and blue paint.

8. The basketballs did not have enough air.

9

Name _____

Read each cause and effect statement. Circle the best ending for each sentence. Circle the clue word (**so**, **because**, **when**) in each sentence, too.

• •

1. The weather forecaster predicted a rainstorm, so . . .

    a. we went outside to play.

    b. the weather forecaster took a vacation.

    c. we went inside.

2. We ate dinner because . . .

    a. it was early.

    b. we were hungry.

    c. the mail carrier did not come.

3. Snow fell all day, so . . .

    a. the roads were closed.

    b. we swam for hours.

    c. people put away their shovels.

4. I forgot to water the vegetable garden, so . . .

    a. we had a big crop of tomatoes.

    b. the plants died.

    c. I played all afternoon.

5. The ice cream melted because . . .

    a. I forgot to put it back in the freezer.

    b. I did my homework too fast.

    c. I forgot my clarinet.

Try this: On a separate piece of paper, write a sentence like those above. Use **because**, **so**, **since**, or **when** in the sentence. Offer three choices to complete each sentence. Be certain that only one of the three choices is the correct answer. Challenge your friends to choose the correct word or phrase to complete each sentence.

Cause and Effect • CD-104551

Name _____

Read the causes and effects below. Match each cause to the correct effect. Write the letter of the effect on the line by the cause.

Causes

_____ 1. Maria ran a long race.

_____ 2. The drought lasted a month.

_____ 3. The electricity went out last night.

_____ 4. Ocean waves pounded the shore.

Effects

a. She could not water her yard.

b. The sandcastle washed away.

c. She was tired.

d. She could not see a thing.

Garden Effects

Read the stories on this page and the next. Fill in the missing causes and effects.

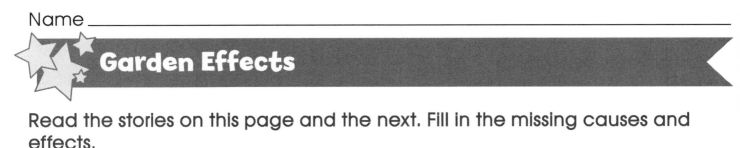

Butterfly Bushes

José and his grandfather wanted to plant a garden that would attract butterflies. They used the Internet to do their research. José discovered that butterflies are born as caterpillars, and caterpillars need to eat a lot of food. Their garden needed plants that caterpillars like to eat. José and his grandfather also discovered that butterflies eat a lot when they grow up. Their garden needed plants that butterflies like to eat.

Cause	**Effect**
1. Caterpillars must eat.	1. _____
2. Butterflies must eat.	2. _____

 **Delilah's Delight**

Delilah had problems all summer. Insects were eating the leaves of her garden plants. She read magazines to find out what would help. She learned that pesticides can be bad for the environment, so Delilah did not want to use them. She also learned that most ladybugs eat insect pests but do not eat garden plants, so ladybugs make perfect plant guards.

Cause	**Effect**
3. _____	3. Delilah did not use pesticides.
4. _____	4. Ladybugs make perfect plant guards.

Garden Effects (cont.)

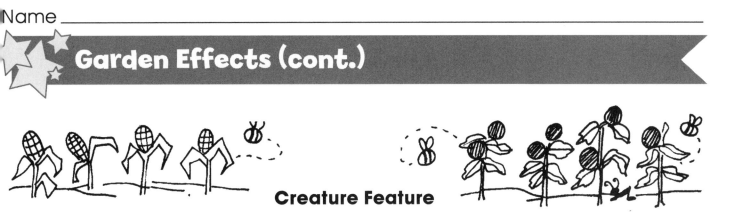

Creature Feature

Diane loves to play her violin in the orchestra. She loves to watch others dance to her music. Diane knows that people are not the only living things that can create beautiful sounds and joyful dances. Crickets chirp when looking for mates. Scout bees dance when they find lots of food. Diane thought about the joys of the insects as she played "Flight of the Bumblebee" at her recital.

Cause	**Effect**
5. _____	5. Crickets chirp.
6. _____	6. Scout bees dance.

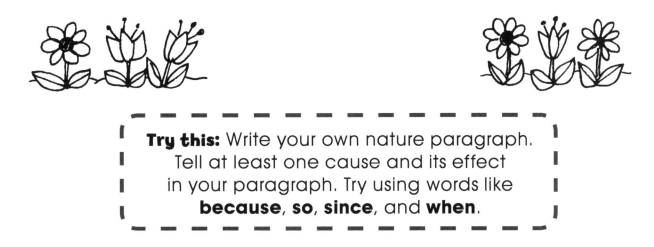

Try this: Write your own nature paragraph. Tell at least one cause and its effect in your paragraph. Try using words like **because**, **so**, **since**, and **when**.

13

Tell Me Why

Look at each picture. Finish the sentence to explain the cause and effect in each one.

1.

_____

_____

because it was raining outside and Dante did not want to get wet.

2.

The dog was very thirsty because

_____

_____

3.

_____

_____

so Heath missed the bus.

4.

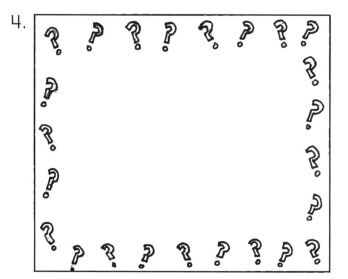

Draw a picture inside this rectangle that clearly shows cause and effect.

Sea Creatures

Circle the cause in each sentence. Draw a line under the effect.

1. Since turtles are often harmed by traps, many types of traps have been outlawed.

2. Because they want to be safe, lobsters walk in single file when they migrate.

3. A manta ray's gills filter plankton from the water so that the ray can get the food it needs.

4. Because killer whales eat fish and small mammals, they have cone-shaped teeth that help them hunt.

5. Because redfish were endangered, fishing for redfish was not permitted.

15

Rhyme Climb

Read the rhymes below. Answer the cause and effect questions on the next page.

1. Simple Simon met a pieman,
   Going to the fair;
   Says Simple Simon to the pieman,
   Let me taste your ware.
   Says the pieman to Simple Simon,
   Show me first your penny;
   Says Simple Simon to the pieman,
   Indeed I have not any.

2. Hey, diddle, diddle,
   The cat and the fiddle,
   The cow jumped over the moon;
   The little dog laughed
   To see such sport,
   And the dish ran away with the spoon.

3. Little Miss Muffet
   Sat on a tuffet,
   Eating her curds and whey;
   There came a big spider,
   Who sat down beside her,
   And frightened Miss Muffet away.

4. Rain, rain, go away,
   Come again another day.
   Little Johnny wants to play.

Rhyme Climb (cont.)

Each number below goes with a poem on the previous page. If the cause is filled in, write the effect. If the effect is filled in, write the cause.

. . . .

Cause

1. _____
   _____
   _____
   _____

2. _____
   _____
   _____
   _____

3. A spider sat down beside Miss Muffet.

4. Johnny wants to play.

Effect

1. Simple Simon did not get any pie.

2. The little dog laughed.

3. _____
   _____
   _____
   _____

4. _____
   _____
   _____
   _____
   _____

17

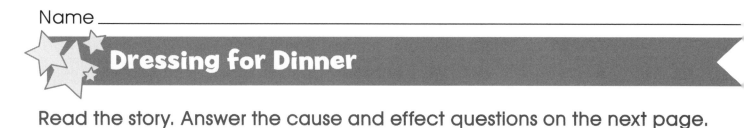

Dressing for Dinner

Read the story. Answer the cause and effect questions on the next page.

• •

Will wants to surprise his dad with a chef's salad. His dad got a promotion at work, so Will wants to celebrate. His dad loves vegetables. Will finished the salad, then opened his cookbook to find the recipe for a special salad dressing.

SALAD DRESSING

2 cups oil

I tablespoon vinegar

I dash of oregano

I pinch of salt

Will worked hard to make the salad dressing. He took out a mixing bowl. He measured 2 cups of vinegar and put it in the bowl. He measured I tablespoon of oil and put it in the bowl. Then he added a dash of oregano and a pinch of salt.

Before his dad got home, Will decided to taste the salad. The fresh vegetables made his mouth water. Will put a little bit of salad in a bowl. He scooped salad dressing and drizzled it across the salad. His tongue tingled as he opened his mouth for the first bite. Will gulped. His eyes watered. He could not believe the taste in his mouth. He felt prickly points dancing from one side of his mouth to the other. He grabbed a glass of water to rinse his mouth.

Will shook his head. "What did I do wrong?" he asked.

  Cause and Effect • CD-104551

Dressing for Dinner (cont.)

Answer the cause and effect questions about Will's salad.

· ·

1. Will made his dad a salad because _____

   _____.

2. Will made a salad instead of a cake because _____

   _____.

3. Will's mouth tingled after eating the salad because _____

   _____.

4. Will's salad dressing tasted funny because _____

   _____.

19

Because I'll Be Responsible

Read the story. Answer the cause and effect questions on the next page.

• •

"I want a dog!" Josh said. He stamped his foot on the ground.

"But you didn't take care of your hamster," his dad said, "and we had to give him away."

"This time it will be different. This time I'll take care of my pet. I promise," said Josh.

"I'll think about it," said Dad. "You have to prove you can take care of a pet, first."

Josh hung his head and shuffled his feet as he walked to his room.

He looked up at his chores list. Josh knew he had to prove that he was responsible, so he finished all his chores for two weeks. He did every chore on the list, just like his Dad wanted him to.

"Now, Dad, please, can we get a dog? You can see how responsible I've been," Josh pleaded.

Dad smiled. "I think the family down the street still has a few puppies left," he said. "Let's go check them out."

"Hurray!" shouted Josh.

Because I'll Be Responsible (cont.)

Complete the cause and effect statements below.

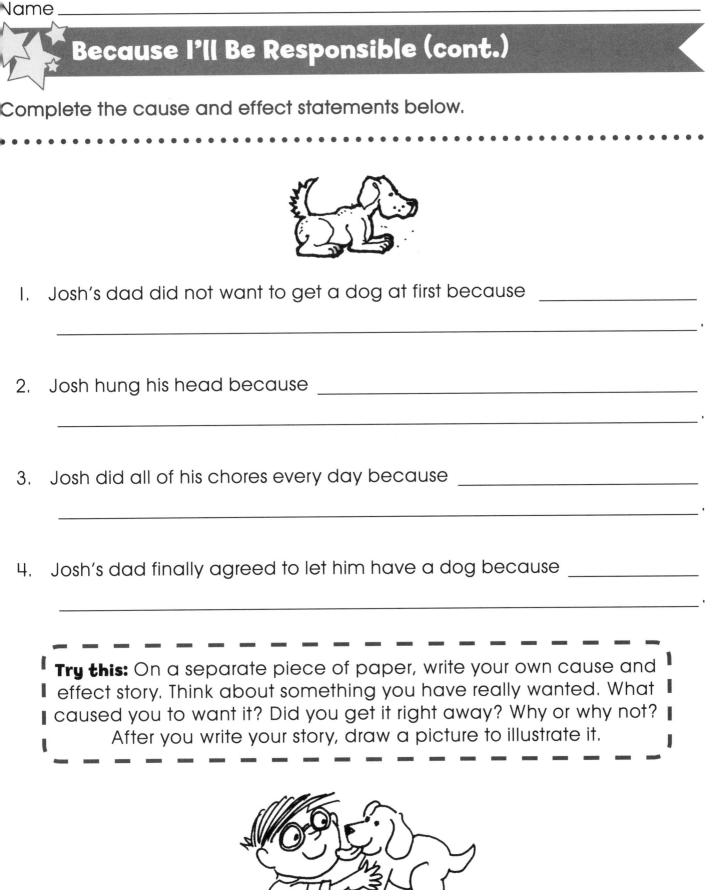

1. Josh's dad did not want to get a dog at first because _____ _____ .

2. Josh hung his head because _____ _____ .

3. Josh did all of his chores every day because _____ _____ .

4. Josh's dad finally agreed to let him have a dog because _____ _____ .

Try this: On a separate piece of paper, write your own cause and effect story. Think about something you have really wanted. What caused you to want it? Did you get it right away? Why or why not? After you write your story, draw a picture to illustrate it.

21

Proverbial Cause

A proverb is a wise old saying. It contains a hidden meaning. Explain what the proverbs, on this page and the next, mean by completing the cause and effect statements. Use the words **because**, **so**, **since**, or **cause** in each of your answers.

• •

Example: Look before you leap.

You should think before you act because the result may cause problems.

1.

This is the straw that broke the camel's back.
One additional little problem _____

_____ .

2.

Don't count your chickens before they've hatched.
Don't count on something to happen before it does because _____

_____ .

Proverbial Cause (cont.)

3.

Don't judge a book by its cover.

_____

_____ because there is more to people than looks.

4.

Don't cry over spilled milk.

Don't worry over little things because _____

_____ .

23

Science Action

Read each description. Answer the cause and effect questions on the next page.

• •

Push Off

Fill a balloon with air. Hold the end closed and then let it go. The balloon will zoom forward as the air escapes. You pushed air into the balloon, and now the air pushes the balloon around as it comes back out.

Pull In

Because a magnet attracts some metals, it can pull a key toward it. A magnet will not pull a rubber band, because a rubber band is not magnetic. Only two magnetic objects will be attracted to each other.

Travel Across

Glaciers are large chunks of ice that slowly move over the land. Glaciers have an effect on the land as they travel. Because glaciers pick up parts of the land as they move, glaciers can carve out large areas. As glaciers melt, they leave behind bits of earth that can build up areas of land.

Circle Around

When the sun heats water, the water evaporates and forms vapor. The vapor forms clouds when it cools. The water droplets fall to the earth as rain. The rain evaporates, and the cycle begins again.

Science Action (cont.)

Circe the correct answer for each question.

1. Glaciers change the land because . . .

   a. there is an equal and opposite re-action for every action.

   b. water drops grow heavy.

   c. they pick up pieces of land as they move.

   d. they are frozen.

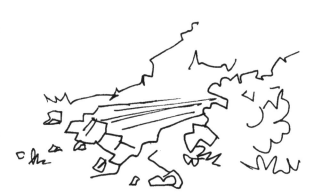

2. If you fill a balloon with air, hold the end, and let it go, it will zoom forward because . . .

   a. it is frozen.

   b. a balloon is a law of motion.

   c. air pushes it.

   d. vapor forms clouds.

3. Water evaporates because . . .

   a. the sun heats up the water.

   b. it is a law of motion.

   c. a magnet attracts metal.

   d. water drops grow heavy.

4. A magnet will pull a key in its direction because . . .

   a. water drops grow heavy.

   b. the magnet and the key are both magnetic.

   c. a rubber band is not made of metal.

   d. it leaves behind something that has been frozen inside.

Name _____

Ulric and his classmates gave speeches, but people in the audience could not hear everything. Help them figure out what was said. Match each effect with the correct cause. Write the answers on the lines by the causes.

Effect

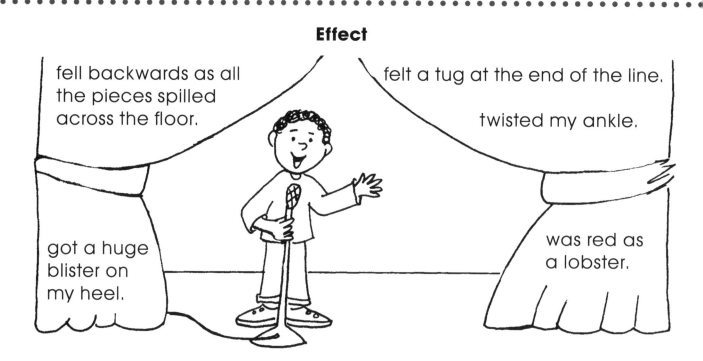

fell backwards as all the pieces spilled across the floor.

felt a tug at the end of the line.

twisted my ankle.

got a huge blister on my heel.

was red as a lobster.

Cause

1. Ulric: We played on the beach all day, but we forgot our sunscreen, so I

_____ .

2. Lu: I skated for hours in my new skates, but there was a hole in my sock, so I _____ .

3. Tia: I used my new fishing rod. I waited for hours. Because I used a good fishing lure, I finally _____ .

4. Ling: I played in a chess tournament. During the third match, someone's dog jumped up on the chess board, and I _____

_____ .

5. Dominique: I ran in six races at camp. Because someone tripped me in the last race, I _____

Speaker Squeaker

Match each cause to the correct effect. Write the answers on the lines by the effects.

• •

Cause

Mom touched the match to the candle.

The bright sun shone right in my eyes.

I pedaled my bike as hard as I could.

I kicked with all my might.

We watered the garden every day.

1. Lena: I held up my mitt, but I could not see the ball.

    Cause:_____

2. Alfred: Then the flame rose high.

    Cause:_____

3. Susan: The flowers grew full and tall.

    Cause:_____

4. Oscar: The wheels turned quickly.

    Cause:_____

5. Quincy: The soccer ball sailed into the goal.

    Cause:_____

Name _____

Read the article. Answer the cause and effect questions below.

• •

In 1980, scientist Tim Berners-Lee was working with software in the Swiss Alps. He wanted to create a way to organize and find information, because it was hard to share information with scientists in different countries. He thought of the World Wide Web.

How did the World Wide Web get its name? Berners-Lee and a coworker tried to think of names. They could not come up with any ideas they liked. Because they needed a name quickly, they came up with the World Wide Web. This name described how information was passed around the world. They planned to think of another name later. However, the World Wide Web caught on quickly and was never changed.

1. Why did Tim Berners-Lee come up with the idea for the World Wide Web?

   _____

   _____

2. Why did Tim Berners-Lee and a coworker decide to use the name World Wide Web? _____

   _____

   _____

3. Why do you think Tim Berners-Lee thought there needed to be a way to organize and find information? _____

   _____

   _____

Out-of-This-World Vacation

Read the advertisement. Answer the cause and effect questions below.

Come join us . . .

. . . for a thrilling once-in-a-lifetime vacation! Hop aboard our luxury space liner and fly to the moon for an adventurous six-day vacation. We know you will love this one because you are thrill-seeking, fun-loving kinds of people. You will love the happy feeling of floating through the air. And, because there is no gravity, your luggage will feel as light as air. Since we will be approximately 221,456 miles (356,399 km) above the earth, you will find the view amazing. We hope you join us for this awesome trip.

Rules and Restrictions:
Due to a decreased amount of fresh air, no smoking will be allowed on the flight. A charge of $8.4 million will be in place due to high fuel costs.

1. Why does the travel agency know people will love this vacation?

    _____

    _____

2. Why will travelers' luggage feel as light as air?

    _____

    _____

3. Why is no smoking allowed?

    _____

    _____

4. Why does the trip cost $8.4 million?

    _____

    _____

Prima Ballerina

Read the story. Write the answers on the lines below to complete the cause and effect statements.

• •

Keisha loved to watch ballet because the dancers flew through the air. They made great leaps and jumps. One day, Keisha decided she wanted to be a ballerina. She practiced standing on her toes all day long. Nothing happened. She practiced leaping across the living room. Nothing happened. She even leaped off the couch! Keisha still did not feel like a ballerina.

Keisha was desperate. She wanted to be a ballerina more than anything else. Finally, she asked her mom to buy her a tutu. Surely that would mean she was a ballerina. She slipped on the tutu and waited. Nothing happened. Keisha sat down on the floor and cried. "Why can't I be a ballerina?" she asked.

Just then, Keisha's mom dropped a paper on her lap. It said "Madame Bleu's Ballerina School" on the front. Keisha beamed from ear to ear. Dance school would help her become a ballerina!

1. Keisha likes to watch ballet because _____

   _____ .

2. Keisha practices standing on her toes and leaping because _____

   _____ .

3. Keisha asks her mom to buy her a tutu because _____

   _____ .

4. Keisha cries because _____

   _____ .

5. Keisha smiles at the end of the story because _____

   _____ .

Name _____

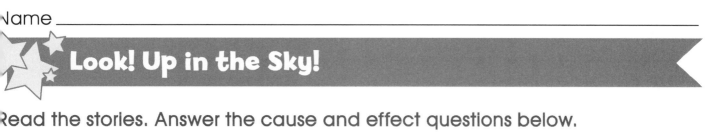

Read the stories. Answer the cause and effect questions below.

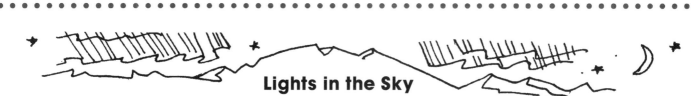

Lights in the Sky

An aurora borealis is one of the brightest night-time lights people have ever seen. It can be caused by particles in the air that reflect light. It can also be caused by huge eruptions of gas on the sun. These eruptions are called solar flares. People often describe an aurora borealis as "light dancing across the sky."

1. How many effects are discussed in this paragraph? _____

2. Explain your answer. What are the effects? _____

    _____

3. How many causes are discussed in this paragraph? _____

4. Explain your answer. What are the causes? _____

    _____

Explosion in the Sky

In 1937, the Hindenburg airship exploded in the sky. For years, people argued about what caused the explosion. Hydrogen gas caused the airship to rise into the sky. At first, people thought that hydrogen gas had caused the explosion. Now, it is believed that a different chemical on the airship made it explode. The chemical might have been a powdered metal.

1. What did people first believe caused the explosion of the Hindenburg?

    _____

    _____

2. What did people later believe caused the explosion of the Hindenburg?

    _____

    _____

  31

Name _____

Read the story. Complete the cause and effect statements on the next page.

• •

Jana scrunched her nose and dove into her bed. Not tomorrow, she thought. The science fair cannot be tomorrow! Jana knew she'd have to give the speech she had prepared to go with her science fair project. She was terrified to speak in front of big crowds. Just thinking about the report made her heart beat faster.

Yolanda burst into Jana's room. "Did you hear?" Yolanda shouted. "We could get a prize for our report tomorrow."

"What do you mean?" asked Jana.

"The City Science Committee is going to all the schools to listen to the reports. They're going to give a big cash prize to the people who win."

"Our family could really use that money," Jana said. "Linda will be finished with high school soon, and the money could help her pay for college."

The next day, Jana and Yolanda set up the equipment to prepare for the report. Jana asked Yolanda to connect all the wiring because Yolanda worked well with electronics.

Jana opened her mouth to speak as Yolanda prepared to show the audience how the experiment worked, but not a single sound came from Jana's mouth. She felt sweat bead up on her palms. Her hands shook. Silence filled the room.

Our family needs the prize money, thought Jana. I know I can do this. Slowly, Jana began to speak. Her hands stopped shaking. She explained to the listeners that the lights in the experiment would light up because they received a charge from the batteries through the wiring. She explained how she and Yolanda had thought of the experiment.

The next day, Yolanda burst into Jana's room again. She was grinning from ear to ear because she was so happy. "Have you heard? It's the best of the best news! We won!"

"I knew we could do it," said Jana. She and Yolanda raced downstairs to tell their mom and dad and older sister.

Light the Lights! (cont.)

Complete the cause and effect statements.

1. Jana did not even want to think about the report because _____
   _____.

2. Jana wanted to win the science competition because _____
   _____.

3. Yolanda connected the wiring because _____
   _____.

4. Jana's hands shook because _____
   _____.

5. Jana began speaking because _____
   _____.

6. The lights in the experiment lit up because _____
   _____.

7. The day after the competition, Jana and Yolanda raced down the stairs
   because _____
   _____.

33

Consequences

Actions have consequences. An action is the cause, and a consequence is the result. For each of the story starters on this page and the next, write a sentence that shows a consequence.

Example: What if Suki Forgot?

a. Suki forgot to write her assignments in her notebook.
Consequence: Suki forgot she had math homework. She did not do it.

b. Suki remembered to write her assignments in her notebook.
Consequence: Suki did all of her homework. She got an A in the class.

I. How Hard Did Shalti Work?

a. Shalti wanted to be part of the school band, but he did not practice.
Consequence: _____

_____

b. Shalti wanted to be part of the school band. He practiced and practiced.
Consequence: _____

_____

  Cause and Effect • CD-104551

Name _____

2. On the Right Path
   a. Tara did not stay with her group on the camp hike.

   Consequence: _____

   _____

   b. Tara stayed with her group on the camp hike.

   Consequence: _____

   _____

3. Chore Score
   a. Julio did not finish his chores.

   Consequence: _____

   _____

   b. Julio finished his chores.

   Consequence: _____

   _____

Try this: Think of something you have done and the consequences of the action. On a separate piece of paper, write a short story that tells what would have happened if you had done the opposite.

Dancing in Rio

Read the story. Answer the cause and effect questions on the next page.

• •

Allen was upset. His parents said they had to go to a wedding in Brazil, and Allen had to go too. It meant two whole weeks away from his friends! Allen thought the wedding would be boring. What was so interesting about Brazil?

When he got to Rio, Allen realized the word boring did not fit anything! The whole country of Brazil was throwing a big party. The celebration was called Carnival. Rio was the center of the party.

There were people in bright clothes everywhere. Everyone danced in the streets. The music was loud and exciting. It made Allen want to dance with the crowd.

Allen was excited for other reasons too. When they left Wisconsin, it was snowing. Down in Brazil it was summer! He could wear shorts and flip-flops.

"Don't go out of my sight!" his mom shouted. The same sights that made Allen happy seemed to make his mom nervous.

The music got louder. It made Allen's heart jump. Mary, his older sister, liked it too. Together, Allen and Mary danced with the music.

That night there was a party. It was for the bride and groom. Everyone was dancing. Allen's heart was still jumping. He watched Mary dance. His sister was good! The bride asked Allen to join them.

"Come out on the dance floor!" she said.

Allen was nervous. Everyone was watching him. He had never danced in front of an audience. No one had been watching him at Carnival.

"Allen, you were a good dancer today. Show everyone your dance steps!" Mary said.

That gave Allen courage. He went out onto the dance floor. Allen danced all night long. At the end of the night, the Brazilians cheered for him.

"You are the best of everyone," they said.

Dancing in Rio (cont.)

Finish the cause and effect statements.

• •

1. Allen did not want to go to Brazil because _____
   _____.

2. Rio did not seem boring because _____
   _____.

3. Allen liked the music at Carnival because _____
   _____.

4. Allen was nervous to dance with the bride and groom because _____
   _____.

5. Allen stopped being nervous when _____.

6. Do you think Allen had a good time? Why or why not? _____
   _____
   _____

37

Sensible Effects

Read each cause statement. Write two effects that make sense for each cause.

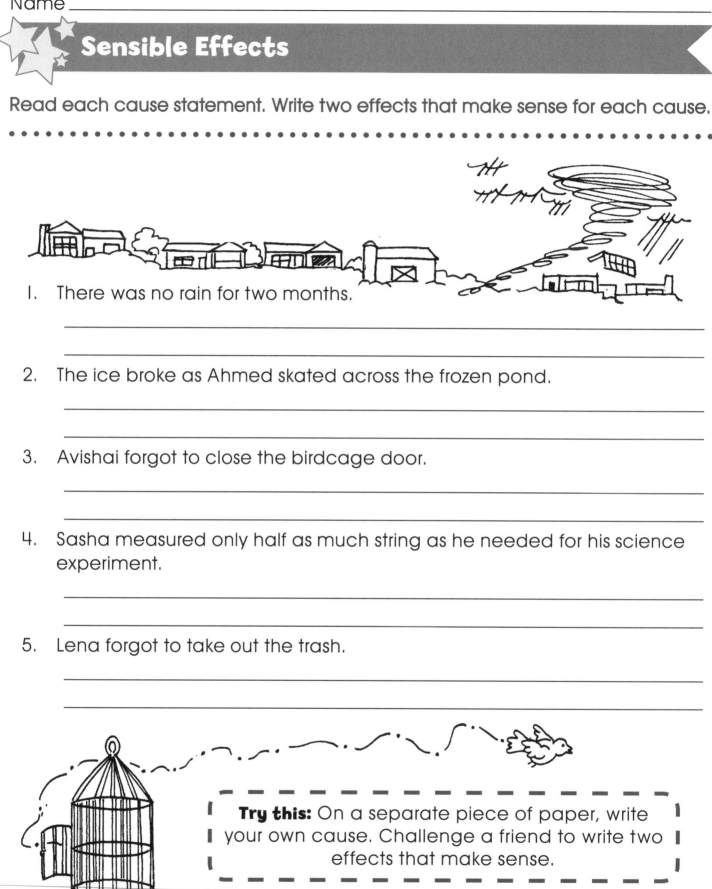

1. There was no rain for two months.

    _____

    _____

2. The ice broke as Ahmed skated across the frozen pond.

    _____

    _____

3. Avishai forgot to close the birdcage door.

    _____

    _____

4. Sasha measured only half as much string as he needed for his science experiment.

    _____

    _____

5. Lena forgot to take out the trash.

    _____

    _____

Try this: On a separate piece of paper, write your own cause. Challenge a friend to write two effects that make sense.

Name _____

Write two causes that make sense for each effect.

1. The candle's flame went out.

    _____

    _____

2. The birds suddenly flew into the trees.

    _____

    _____

3. The flowers in the garden drooped.

    _____

    _____

4. Our dog dashed to the front door.

    _____

    _____

5. Our dog panted.

    _____

    _____

6. The boat moved across the lake.

    _____

    _____

Try this: On a separate piece of paper, write your own effect. Challenge a friend to write two causes that make sense.

All Arrows Point to Effect

An effect is found in each circle. Complete each circle by writing a cause on each line pointing to the effect.

1. I received an excellent grade on my paper.

2. We had the best tomato crop ever.

All Arrows Point to Effect (cont.)

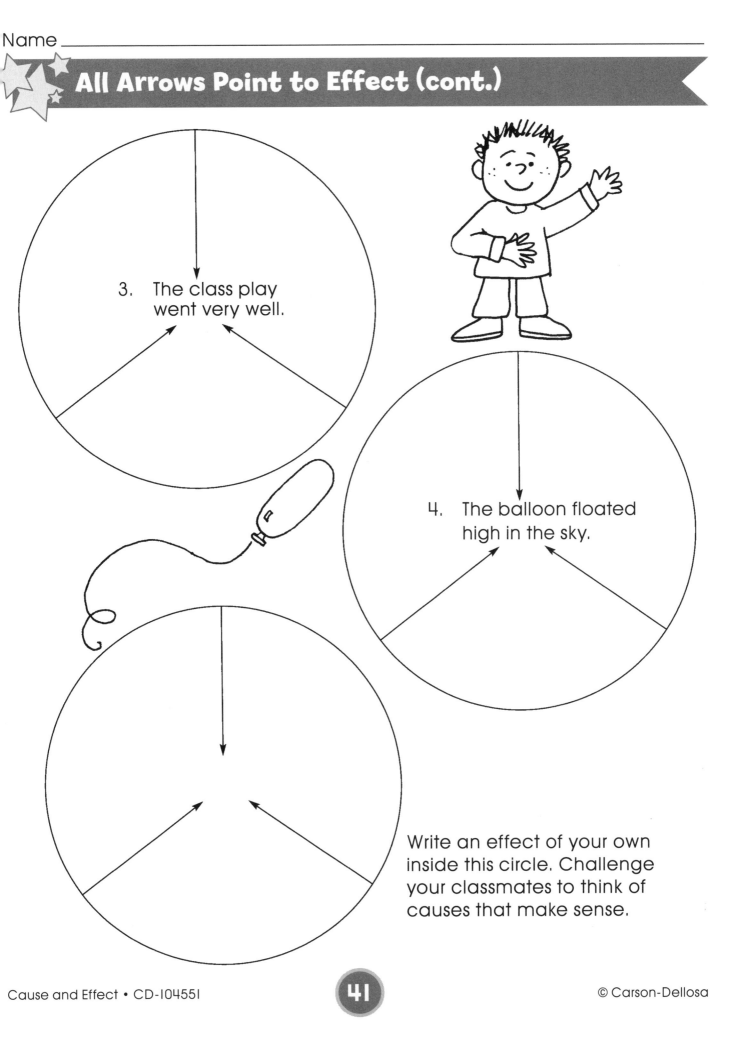

3. The class play went very well.

4. The balloon floated high in the sky.

Write an effect of your own inside this circle. Challenge your classmates to think of causes that make sense.

41

The Greatest Gift

Read the story. Answer the cause and effect questions on the next page.

Rena dabbed her paintbrush across her palette. She brushed the color across the canvas. *I'll never be able to do it,* she thought. *I can't paint the picture of the woods.* She gazed at the painting on the wall of the art studio.

"Rena," said her art teacher. "What you've done here is beautiful! You have such talent. You're one of my best students because you have such an unusual style."

Rena shook her head. "Maybe, but my work will never look like that." She looked again at the painting hanging on the wall.

When Rena walked in the door at home, her little brother grabbed her by the arm. "Rena, Rena, will you make a picture for Grandpa's party? I wrote a poem for him, but I want to put it with a great big picture. And I want you to do it because you're such a great artist."

Rena smiled. "Okay, Oscar. Grab all those old pictures from the box."

Oscar skipped out of the room. A few minutes later, he dashed in, carrying Grandpa's photos. It was hard to piece them together because they were all torn, and they were faded.

At the art studio, Rena laid the torn and faded photos across a table so she could arrange them in a special way. For weeks, Rena worked with her paints on a big canvas. She placed every stroke and chose every color with great care.

At Grandpa's party, Oscar read his poem. Then Rena gave Grandpa the painting. Tears filled Grandpa's eyes. "The poem was wonderful, and the painting . . . the painting shows my old friends and my old neighborhood in a way that makes me feel as though I'm there all over again. Rena, you've shown me how special all these people have been in my life. You and Oscar are wonderful."

The Greatest Gift (cont.)

Answer the cause and effect questions.

. . . .

1. Why did Rena's art teacher like Rena's work?

    _____

    _____

    _____

2. Why did Oscar want Rena to paint a picture for Grandpa?

    _____

    _____

    _____

3. Why was it hard to piece together Grandpa's old photos?

    _____

    _____

    _____

4. Why did Grandpa cry when he saw Rena's painting?

    _____

    _____

    _____

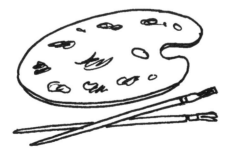

43

Name _____

The Giant Wave

Read the article. Complete the cause and effect statements below.

• •

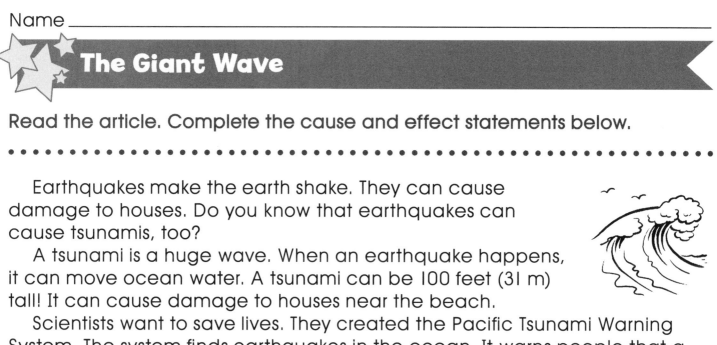

Earthquakes make the earth shake. They can cause damage to houses. Do you know that earthquakes can cause tsunamis, too?

A tsunami is a huge wave. When an earthquake happens, it can move ocean water. A tsunami can be 100 feet (31 m) tall! It can cause damage to houses near the beach.

Scientists want to save lives. They created the Pacific Tsunami Warning System. The system finds earthquakes in the ocean. It warns people that a big wave may be coming. People can seek safety before the wave hits.

1. Tsunamis are caused by _____.

2. A tsunami causes _____.

3. Experts have created a warning system because _____

    _____.

4. The warning system helps people because _____

    _____.

Washed Away

Read the article. Then answer the questions below.

• •

Erosion causes rocks and soil to be broken down. It can be caused by water, wind, ice, or gravity. People often think of erosion by water because it can be so noticeable. One famous example of erosion is Niagara Falls. These falls used to be 7 miles (11km) away from their current position but have moved over the years because of erosion. Water and small pieces of rock have worn away the cliffs and caused the flow of water to slowly move backward. Because some of the rock is softer, it is worn away first. If you were to take all the water away from the falls, you would see that the top of the rock sticks out farther than the bottom. This is because the bottom rock is softer.

Erosion is always at work. The more water that flows over rocks, the more the rocks erode. At Niagara Falls, they have tried to slow down the erosion by stopping some of the water from reaching the falls. So, only some of the water that should be eroding the rock is doing its job. However, the falls will continue to slowly erode. People can try to slow down erosion, but they will never stop it.

1. Why have the Niagara Falls moved?

    _____

    _____

2. Why does the top of Niagara Falls stick out farther than the bottom?

    _____

    _____

3. Why have people tried to stop water from going over the falls?

    _____

    _____

4. What do you think will eventually happen to Niagara Falls?

    _____

    _____

Answer Key

Page 4
Draw Lines: 1. a; 2. c; 3. b

Page 5
1. cause, effect; 2. effect, cause;
3. effect, cause; 4. cause, effect;
5. effect, cause; 6. cause, effect;
7. effect, cause

Pages 6–7
Inside camp cabin: She loves tennis classes. People are nice. She likes riding horses. Inside apartment building: She misses her tennis court. She misses her grandma and their tennis matches. She misses frozen yogurt.

Page 8
Draw Lines: 1. d; 2. b; 3. f; 4. a; 5. c;
6. g; 7. e

Page 9
Draw Lines: 1. g; 2. d; 3. b; 4. h; 5. c;
6. e; 7. a; 8. f

Page 10
Circle: 1. so, c; 2. because, b; 3. so, a;
4. so, b; 5. because, a

Page 11
1. c; 2. a; 3. d; 4. b

Pages 12–13
Answers vary. Examples: 1. Jose's garden needed plants for caterpillars. 2. Jose's garden needed plants for butterflies. 3. Pesticides can be bad for the environment.
4. Delilah used ladybugs in her garden. 5. Crickets look for mates.
6. Scout bees find lots of food.

Page 14
Answers vary. Examples: 1. Dante put on a rain coat; 2. there was no water in his bowl; 3. Heath was late; 4. Answers vary depending on student picture.

Page 15
Circle: 1. turtles are often harmed by traps; 2. they want to be safe; 3. A manta ray's gills filter plankton from the water; 4. killer whales eat fish and small mammals; 5. redfish were endangered; Underline: 1. many types of traps have been outlawed;
2. lobsters walk in single file when they migrate; 3. the ray can get the food it needs; 4. they have cone-shaped teeth that help them hunt; 5. fishing for redfish was not permitted

Pages 16–17
Answers vary. Examples: 1. Simple Simon did not have a penny. 2. The cow jumped over the moon. 3. It frightened Miss Muffet away. 4. Little Johnny told the rain to go away.

Pages 18–19
Answers vary. Examples: 1. he wanted to celebrate his dad's new job; 2. his dad loves vegetables; 3. it tasted bad; 4. he did not follow the recipe

Page 20–21
Answers vary. Examples: 1. he did not think Josh would take care of a dog; 2. he was sad he could not have a dog; 3. he wanted to prove he was responsible; 4. Josh proved he could be responsible

Pages 22–23
Answers vary. Examples: 1. can cause big problems; 2. you could be disappointed; 3. don't judge people by looks; 4. they are not worth worrying about

Pages 24–25
Circle: 1. c; 2. c; 3. a; 4. b

Page 26
1. was red as a lobster; 2. got a huge blister on my heel; 3. felt a tug at the end of the line; 4. fell backwards as all the pieces spilled across the floor; 5. twisted my ankle

Page 27
1. The bright sun shone right in my eyes. 2. Mom touched the match to the candle. 3. We watered the garden every day. 4. I pedaled my bike as hard as I could. 5. I kicked with all my might.

Page 28
Answers vary. Examples: 1. so scientists could share information; 2. it described how information was passed; 3. it was hard to share information with scientists in different countries without the WWW

Page 29
Answers vary. Examples: 1. They are thrill-seeking, fun-loving people. 2. There is no gravity. 3. A decreased amount of fresh air. 4. High gas prices.

Page 30
Answers vary. Examples: 1. the dancers fly through the air; 2. she wants to be a ballerina; 3. she thinks it will make her a ballerina; 4. she was not a ballerina; 5. she is going to school to become a ballerina

Page 31
Answers vary. Examples: Lights in the Sky: 1. 2; 2. aurora borealis is one of the brightest night-time lights, it is like light dancing across the sky; 3. 2; 4. charged particles, solar flares; Explosions in the Sky: 1. hydrogen; 2. powdered metal

Pages 32–33
Answers vary. Examples: 1. she was terrified to speak in front of big crowds; 2. she wanted the prize money; 3. she worked well with electronics; 4. she was very nervous to speak; 5. she knew her family needed the money; 6. the charge from the batteries went through the wiring; 7. they wanted to tell their family they won

Pages 34–35

Answers vary. Examples: 1a. Shalti did not get to be on the band. 1b. Shalti got to be in band. 2a. Tara got lost. 2b. Tara got to see the wilderness. 3a. Julio did not get to go out and play. 3b. Julio got extra dessert after dinner.

Pages 36–37

Answers vary. Examples: 1. he thought it would be boring; 2. there was a party; 3. it was loud; 4. he never danced when people were watching; 5. his sister told him he was a good dancer; 6. Yes, his heart jumped from excitement.

Page 38

Answers vary. Examples: 1. The plants did not grow. Everything was very dry. 2. Ahmed had to stop skating. Ahmed was scared he would fall in. 3. The bird flew out of the cage. Avishai was sad. 4. Sasha could not complete his experiment. Sasha had to measure the string again. 5. Lena's parents were mad. The house smelled like garbage.

Page 39

Answers vary. Examples: 1. A strong breeze came in through the window. 2. The cat chased the birds. The dog chased the birds. 3. I forgot to water the flowers. It was autumn. 4. Our dog heard a noise. The mail carrier came to the door. 5. We played fetch for hours. It was hot outside. 6. We paddled hard. The wind blew hard in our sails.

Pages 40–41

Answers vary. Examples: 1. I studied all night. I knew all of the answers. I spelled the words correctly. 2. We watered the plants. We got good soil. We planted the seeds at the right time. 3. We knew all of our lines. We practiced every day. We knew all of the dance steps. 4. We filled the balloon with helium. I forgot to tie the balloon down. The wind blew the balloon around.

Pages 42–43

Answers vary. Examples: 1. She had a unique style. 2. She was a good painter. 3. They were torn and faded. 4. He remembered all of his old friends and really liked it.

Page 44

Answers vary. Examples: 1. earthquakes; 2. damage; 3. they want to save lives; 4. it can warn them when tsunamis are coming

Page 45

Answers vary. Examples: 1. erosion; 2. The bottom is softer and erode faster. 3. They want to slow erosion. 4. Niagara Falls will keep eroding, because you cannot stop erosion.